HOW TO HAVE A

GREAT DAY OFF

SHEILA COHEN

Preface

How To Have A Great Day Off is for anyone who has ever found themselves wasting a precious day off work. It's easy to do. Free days — whether you have them every week or just here and there — can easily be pulled in so many directions that they become nothing at all. A day off can be a blank diary page that remains blank, or it can be a whole day of procrastination. Or it can be the restorative, productive and inspirational day that powers the rest of your week. This book is about making that valuable day work for you.

Sheila Cohen, a former teacher and careers adviser, says it's time to take charge of your time. In a witty whip through the delusions, discoveries and drawer fluff of the time she suddenly had after downsizing her working week, she offers a new solution. Name your day.

Outlining 12 day-types, this book encourages you to think differently about your Day Off — and most importantly, how to make it happen.

Acknowledgements

I am grateful to my family, work colleagues and friends for their interest, support and ideas during the preparation of this book.

Contents

Chapter 4 Proper Days Out (page 98)

Day Out with Friends-*a day out with others*

Explore By Yourself Day-*a day out exploring new places by yourself*

Chapter 5 Days Going Wrong (page 114)

Motivational Tricks-*how to get back on track*

Unavoidable Intrusions-*how to deal with interruptions, weather, the seasonal calendar*

The Cinderella Factor-*how to have a smooth transition back to work*

Introduction

A few years ago, I down-sized my job to four days a week. At a late stage in my career, I had decided that while I would continue to work, enough was enough, and I would take some time for myself.

In the weeks leading up to my first Day Off, in the kitchen at work I overheard a young colleague talking about what she had done on her Day Off. "Oh! Nothing much. A bit of this and that," she'd replied glumly, and that was it. Stunned, I removed myself quickly from the kitchen and shuffled back to my desk. A Day Off! Nothing much! I could not accept this state of affairs.

I'm a planner and a perfectionist — I'll admit that right now — but surely this just isn't right, I thought. The idea of my forthcoming free day was an Aladdin's cave. I wondered how much I could carry out of it. In these early Days Off, I felt like I feel at weekends but better. I remember waking up on the first one feeling euphoric. Suddenly, far from being pushed along through endless tasks of work, I was my own boss for a day. Everybody else was at work! Ha. Free of any routine, I could do anything. Perhaps I would rediscover the person I had been before I was a worker, or even the person I was going to be in the future. I could think creatively and problem-solve. I would keep weekend chores confined to the weekend; there must be contrast in order to maintain the mystery of the Aladdin's Cave, I wisely instructed myself. I would keep my day special, and it would be wonderful.

That was the first heady day of freedom. After that it was pure, existential terror. With so many conflicting aims, I floundered stumbling through days of doing extra housework, planning everything under the sun, impulsively racing to the shops or sitting trying to do nothing (something I've never been terribly good at, as you'll no doubt come to realise during the following chronicles). The down-side of being boss for the day is that if you don't get what you want from it, there is no one else to blame. I often found myself pulled in so many directions that I went back to work discontented and annoyed at myself.

The plight of my glum colleague was now all too familiar. It seems that the thought of a Day Off often makes us happier than the reality. We want to go off into a magic wonderland for the day, but know perfectly well that there are heaps of more mundane tasks that we will end up doing instead. I wondered if this "total escape" myth is a folk-memory from our 19th century industrial past when whole coach-loads of workers used to spill out into to the new sea-side resorts specially created for them to have a day of fun in contrast to their punishing work-days.

Why is it that if we don't designate a Day Off for a fixed purpose - like a wedding, or waiting in for a fridge to be delivered - we tend just to drift? We plan our work days and our weekends, but there seems to be a strange blind-spot when it comes to planning Days Off. I suppose being able to relax is such a luxury that the idea of planning anything doesn't enter our heads - but as my colleague and I both discovered, it turns out that doing "nothing much" isn't always as relaxing as it's cracked up to be;

particularly if you have that window of free time every week.

I've always found it helpful to write my worries down, so I started to write regularly about what had gone well, what badly on my Days Off. I noticed that I had tried out all sorts of ways to use the day. One day while writing, I had an idea: why not *name* the day, and establish it as a type of day you could *choose*? I made up names for the kinds of Days Off I'd tried out, and finally realised that it was actually the act of naming of the day itself which determined whether it worked well or not.

This book is the result of my many experiments with my regular day off over the period of a year — and of the experience of a former teacher and careers adviser in encouraging personal achievement.

I admitted to myself early on that underlying the whole project was my own need for a structure to the day — and the need, in fact, to use many of the work-skills which you are supposed to leave in the work-place. But as I continued to chronicle how my various named days had gone, and eventually honed them into the 12 you see in the Contents page, it became a project to help others.

This is isn't a scientific self-help book, but a friendly companion for those taking their days into their own hands. I hope you can learn from my discoveries and mistakes, and I hope you laugh at them as well. I'm aware that my needs and experiences will likely be different to yours, so I'd encourage you, fellow adventurers, to take the concept and run with it. Try my day-types off-the-peg if you want to, or have a go at creating your own.

And before you say it, I know there's a time and place for doing "nothing much". That's a Whatever You Feel Like day.

Chapter 1 - Multi-focus Days

I've called the types of day in this chapter *multi-focus* because during the day you will engage in a series of different unrelated activities rather than mainly focussing on a single activity as in the next chapter, Single-focus Days.

Multi-focus Days are mainly home-based. They work better when staying at home feels good. They are for useful things...useful to you. They must restore you by putting your mind at rest that your life is ordered and can support your working life, but they must also inspire you, provide rest and a change from working days.

They can be specifically tailored to catch up, or to do or plan a number of activities you never get round to. Alternatively, they can be days when you switch off your usual home reflexes and float about, doing what feels right at the time. Which of the four Multi-focus types of day you choose for your Day Off will depend on your current needs, mood and energy levels.

I asked some work-colleagues how they handled a Day Off. Jane was the most honest. She said she thought about all sorts of things she wanted to do, then on the day usually sat on the settee with the cats and the newspapers until lunch-time, then frittered the afternoon away. The day started in bliss but after lunch there was a serious slump and this is perhaps why the drab phrase "A bit of this and that" summed it up. The suggested day-types in this Chapter will prevent you from falling into a drab pattern, repeated on all your Days Off.

Of course it is true that most of us at home on a Day Off would be doing a bit of *pottering*. What we must not forget is that we have an in-built need to potter. Pottering means just going from one little ordering activity to another. Even if Jane called the afternoon *frittering,* she was probably pottering: gently picking the dead leaves off the geraniums, tidying the window-sill, nothing radical. You get real pleasure from these small things. Even staying in a hotel, I find myself enjoying tidying up.

Days Off should be neither wholly indulgent nor

just a chance to do more housework: this chapter will show you how to tailor your day to your needs and enjoy every minute of it. Regard the day as a sacred space to re-balance yourself and your affairs. The examples I give in this chapter are necessarily my own. You will put lots of your own different and varied activities into these Multi-focus Days.

Catch-Up Day

You may have been out and about at the weekend or several weekends in a row, or you may have returned from holiday, and the basic maintenance chores of cleaning, washing, food-shopping have gone undone. What you need is a whole day to get straight: a Catch Up Day. It seems a shame to spend a Day Off on this. You may feel disorientated. The sun may be shining and you'll be tempted to rush out somewhere on impulse. Don't do it. Instead just remember this is still a holiday. It's free time for YOU. You have decided to use it to catch up and sort yourself out.

Having committed to the type of Day Off it is, stick to your purpose. But don't worry, it is not all drudgery.

If everyone else is at work and you have the house to yourself you will have peace to think, plan and do. You may not be conscious of it, but at weekends, as you try to do your maintenance, you are fitting around the needs of others. Husbands, wives, partners will ease agendas in at odd moments, children will constantly want your time, teenagers may not be around but are always a worry in their absence, elderly relatives know you're around and phone just as you're getting out the cleaning stuff. While you are at home free from interruption from others the necessary chores will be done faster and better. But also *your mind will be free*. While scrubbing away at the sink, you may suddenly remember the title of a book you want to read or that you need to buy a better kind of cleaning product. You can immediately make a note of things to attend to in the future.

So that this day does not feel like work, you can create a great programme for yourself, combining essentials and desirables. Today your aim is to restore not only your sense of order and control but your physical health. So, as well as rushing around, you need to rest. It is tempting to get carried away as if you had infinite time, but you have to remind yourself constantly that jobs cannot all be done thoroughly. Sometimes I've made a martyr of myself, and other times I've been really lazy. Neither works. For the day to work properly, you need to include spells of relaxation and rest: listening to music, radio, watching TV, reading, whatever you want. If you have to go out food-shopping, you can still enjoy the outing as the shops are quieter.

So where do you start? I'd use the early part of the day to walk round the house making lists of possible and unavoidable activities for my Catch Up Day. I would then put them in the order I'd enjoy best, and number them. Alternatively you can sort them into AM, PM, or AM 1, AM2, PM1, PM2 or further subdivisions. Sometimes I've included estimated times. Before getting stuck in, I'd put in a final treat for about 4.00pm, whatever you'd really like to do. I'd remember to put *flowers* on the shopping list. Flowers are my treat after housework and make the work visible. I'd also work out an easy dinner as I wouldn't want to start cooking at the end of a Catch Up Day.

So off you go, and work your way through the list. Tick jobs off as you go along. The bedroom may not get hoovered. You may need to revise the list, but you will go through the day with a sense of purpose. If at times you feel you are grinding through thankless chores, remember that tomorrow morning you will be walking about in a more pleasant place. You could also remind yourself that as the working week goes on you will certainly *not* want to do major household tasks in the evening. And what about all those ideas you've had? They will all be written down and stored for another Day Off. A fabulous Catch Up Day will leave you feeling refreshed, in control, and quite happy to return to work.

Lesson Learnt

You won't feel the benefit until the next day.

Patchwork Day

A Patchwork Day is also a mixture of activities. It is different from a Catch Up Day in that you do not need so urgently to catch up but you have a number of things stored up which your Day Off can easily accomplish. "Patchwork" implies variety, and the jobs you will do will not be related to one another. As you move from one to another you will sense the contrast and feel glad to be able to work in so many different ways. I'd say this is the most common type of Day Off because people resort to bits and pieces when they have not had time to decide what they *really need* to use the free day for. A patchwork is better than "bits and pieces" because its little squares of cloth have been carefully placed and sewn together so that you can enjoy the contrasts between them. You will do the same with your tasks. The difference is in your intentions, the design of your day, which gives you choice and power over your free time. The day may be led by something essential, like preparing for an imminent event. A friend might be coming round in the evening and you need to cook something, or guests may be coming for the weekend and you will have to sort bedding. However, although essential, these preparations need not take over your day. If you allow this to happen, you will no longer have the feeling of a Day Off: limit the preparation time, keep it simple and write down other things you want or need to do.

It may be that your essential activity is paying off your credit-card and some other bills, but you will still have lots of time left. If you are super-organised, you will have an on-going list of "To Do's" to select from to fill the day. If not, try walking around the house, as in Catch Up Day. As you go from room to room opening cupboards, drawers, wardrobe, you will see things just begging to be done. You might even trip over a bag, or catch a whiff of something awful in the fridge or remember you need batteries or cooking oil. You can also leaf through your diary as a way of bringing to mind what would be useful to get on with.

A patchwork format allows you to have a balance of activities. If you sit for too long, you feel stiff and if you exert for too long you get tired, so you can plan the tasks in slices of *active* and *quiet.* You can build the contrast into your list. First make a list, then draw a cloud shape beside the quiet activities and a zig-zag beside the active ones. Then you can see if you have too much of one or the other and chop out some for another time. It is better to leave the fine detail of the patchwork until the day because only then will you know how energetic or otherwise you feel, what the weather is like and so on.

The Old Half-and-Half Day

We have been brought up to think that some things we do out of duty and other things for pure pleasure and that the first category is better done first. A colleague at work says she runs all her Days Off like this : hard work then reward. You can imagine it: in the morning she slaves away and in the afternoon puts her feet up. To me this is too simplistic and I've never been able to operate a day like this, but let's explore it anyway because its an easy formula.

What kind of activity would you put in the morning: extra housework, clearing out cupboards, looking at your bank statements? And to reward yourself in the afternoon: reading a magazine or novel, planning a holiday, drinking hot chocolate, having a luxurious bath, going out for a walk, going into town. I'm bored already. First of all, I'd enjoy clearing out a cupboard. Second, I can only read magazines for a short time, and third, I'd only look at bank statements if I thought I'd been defrauded.

What if we turn the work-then-reward formula on its head? In the morning you would relax and in the afternoon do what you know needs doing. My daughter's boyfriend said that he normally spends the first half of the day lazing around and finally, feeling guilty, gets on with his "to dos" in the afternoon. Frankly, I find this equally uninspiring, and with both of these ways of doing half-and-half, you'd end up getting into a rut, with all your Days-Off feeling the same. The old half-and-half housewife's day is no longer useful. I think that patchwork is a winning format because of the contrasts of duty and relaxation you can build in *throughout* the day, making every Day Off different from the one before.

However, as in Catch Up Day, even though you may have been sitting down for some of the day, and not flogging yourself to death, your activities may all have been too sensible and useful rather than pleasurable in themselves. Sometimes I've worked harder on my Day Off off than when I'm at work! You also want to feel *inspired* on your Patchwork Day, so don't forget to programme into the patchwork activities which you find inspirational.

Lesson Learnt

The better the design of your Patchwork, the less the tasks feel like chores.

Lightning Fix-It Day

Where are your nail scissors? On this kind of day you can find them in the first five minutes. Why doesn't your CD player work? You can look at it properly and see if it's had it or can be repaired. So many little problems can be ironed out. This day brings amazing results and is great fun too. The idea is that by the end of the day a large number of tasks you never get round to finally get done and you feel you're walking on air. They must be things which can be fixed relatively easily and quickly.

First of all you need to make a long list of tasks which fall under the heading of " This has been irritating me for ages." What gets you through the day is speed and focus. If you collect all these tedious little jobs into one day and package them as "Lightning Fix-It", you can sell them to yourself and storm your way through. A button could be sewn on. CDs put back in their covers, the frosting-up freezer could be back to normal at last when you manage to find the manual. Ways of generating your list could be walking round the house with a pencil and notebook, looking at your diary forward or backwards, opening a cupboard or filing cabinet.

When you've got the list of tasks, write down beside them roughly how long each will take. The idea is to have a minimum of 20 lasting no longer than 20 minutes each. And I suggest you *do not put them in priority order*: *they must all be done in the random order in which they find themselves.* Not even a pleasant balance. Sometimes you even have to change your clothes which is normally a pain in the neck but in this context really makes you laugh, like an obstacle-race. Don't reward yourself until the end. Grab a sandwich. I can't remember how I invented this day, but here's my report on how the first one went and what I learnt from it.

My First Lightning Fix It Day

" I got a notebook and pencil and wrote tasks prompted by looking round. I felt good for actually defining tasks and felt the day would be quite interesting and varied. I had 28 of them. I resolved to do them in the order I found them. I really wanted to get ahead. I actually managed 26 with a bit of cheating but got very tired by 4.00PM and realised three important points:

- I had not admitted to myself that clearing out my tops drawer was the most important and had not got to it by 4.00PM and then could not face it.

- I needed some shopping and went out later to the supermarket and got even more tired

- I had felt so ambitious about getting so many things done I forgot I was recovering from a bad cold Although I had got a lot done, I felt horribly tired."

It is important to emphasise that to run a successful Lightning Fix-It Day, you have to be feeling very energetic. Although you originally think that the tasks are all equally irritating, you should ask yourself before you start which of them, if it didn't get done, would annoy you most and put an asterisk beside it. Don't do it first...maybe second or third because the day is meant to be fun and it might put you off. Hide it high up on the list and don't make a meal of it. Alternatively, if it's a task which will require thought and persistence, it may have to go in a Patchwork Day or even need a day to itself in the Single Focus category in the next Chapter. Nothing must interfere with the momentum of this day, so if you have to go out, do this last, but it's really better if you stay in. This is a very good type of Day Off for winter.

The fun comes when you declare war on indecision and procrastination.

Once I swooped round, and my eye alighted on a

hideous corner in the lounge where an ancient table was shrouded in a prim lacy cloth and a wobbly lamp sat preening itself, in prime position for five years. I did not let it know its fate there and then but wrote its name UGLY BOY LAMP in capitals: his days were numbered. He was first on the list. I couldn't wait to put him in the charity shop bag under the bed and made sure I left enough time at the end of the day to deliver him. The longest sigh of relief comes at the end of a Lightning Fix-It Day. I gave this section to a male friend to read, someone who is a chronic procrastinator, and he told me that after reading it he'd cleaned out all his kitchen cupboards in one day.

We have seen in the first three of these Multi-focus Days how the formats you choose direct you through the activities you have prioritized as useful to you with built-in spells of relaxation and enjoyment. Because you have laid out a plan, you feel in charge, with no feelings of guilt about wasting the day or missing out on self-indulgence.

Now, you are right to think that these first three Multi-focus days I have described are not the kind of

Days Off you thought you'd be having: they sound too much like hard work! We are not always able to be like this and sometimes want a gentler approach. The Day which follows still contains a variety of activities, but provides a totally different kind of experience, allowing you to *feel* rather than *think* your way through the day.

Lesson Learnt

Undertake only if feeling reasonably energetic, and don't hide a really weighty task in your list.

Whatever You Feel Like Day

In a Whatever You Feel Like Day, you just *do* things and the day takes care of itself. You do not look at the clock or at a list, but instead just instinctively move from one activity to the next. "Feeling" is the operative word and all through the day you pay attention to how you feel physically. Basically as the day begins, you say to yourself:

"OK, what do I feel like doing right now, this moment?", and continue asking this question all day.

You may have thought by its title that the day was about doing whatever you *want,* but "want" implies no restrictions and gives the impression of doing something whimsical or daring and possibly just one activity for the whole day, whereas the emphasis is on "feeling" in this type of day. Being a heavy-duty planner, I discovered this new way of going about things, as a reaction against my usual procedure and wrote this report about how it went. The term "mindful" is frequently used now to express this concept of paying special attention to whatever small activity you are engaged in, so that you are only thinking of one thing at a time.

Escape from the Clock

"I don't really know what the time is. I stayed in bed reading, thinking, watching TV. I had a plate of cereal. Now I've got up, had a shower and got dressed. I feel I want to go out. I still don't know or care what the time is. I might go to the supermarket. I see on the wall that we need washing powder and kitchen roll, so that's good enough for me......."
Here's what happened next:

"I drove into town but decided to go to a different supermarket. Everything was unfamiliar. I found I was not in the mood for shopping. Even so, I noticed various pleasant things about this supermarket: it was small, it had a fish-counter and there was a good selection of meat. I bought the two items and took them to the car. It was a fresh spring day and the sun was warm. I had the lovely sense of everything being possible which quite often accompanies spring. As I made my way into town, I felt it might be coffee-time so I went into a café and bought two postcards, not even very nice ones, so that I could write to two people and not feel awkward on my own. Isn't it funny how you're invisible when you're on your own? Nobody looks at you. Anyway I drank the coffee, wrote the cards and went on my way.

Exploring further along the road, I discovered that the charity shop had been refurbished and was now selling only books and music...what a great chance to get rid of some! I wandered in and saw a few titles. As I said, I wasn't in the mood for shopping. But I did see some bright yellow wrapping paper which I bought. Next, I found myself in the old-fashioned ironmonger's shop destined to buy the two little plastic trays I've needed for about a year. I really went in there because I wanted to breathe in the re-assuring old smell of the wooden floor mixed with soap powder and fertilizer. I took my time, indulging in the past, looking at all the kitchen essentials. I carried on to the delicatessen guessing I'd need to eat at some point, and bought a lovely little pork pie with a slice of apple on top. Next door, there was a new shop selling coffee and tea, so I spent some time with the owner discussing his career, taking in the aroma, and bought some ground coffee. I hadn't put on my watch so I didn't know the time but I suddenly felt hungry smelling the fish and chips from the van, so I walked quickly back to my car and drove home.

It was still sunny, so I fetched a blanket, put it on the bench outside and put my pork pie on a tray with a glass of milk and munched listening to a thrush high on a tree with the pale blue sky behind. I shivered as the sun went behind a cloud and felt too cold to be out, so I went in and sat at the window reading my historical novel with a nice cup of tea. I was suddenly overcome with tiredness so I went to lie down and fell asleep immediately. When I awoke I felt really energetic, so I buzzed around, hoovering and tidying until I was sweaty. Time for a scented bath. Emerging from the bath I saw it was dark *so I looked at the clock for the first time:* 6.00PM! Husband due back at 6.15. No dinner ready or even planned. Now I don't want to go into it, but things went downhill at this point and the evening did not have the carefree *whatever you feel like* mood of the rest of the day."

Writing this report, I was amazed at how much more enjoyment had come from *not knowing the time and not planning anything.* I really had done whatever I'd felt like for the whole day. It had been a perfectly formed mini-holiday. Just a note of caution: all this *whatever you feel like* can be thrilling or relaxing but you need to think about the evening so you can eat properly, wind down, sleep well and ease yourself back into your work routine. It's probably best on these days to create a block of time within which the Whatever Rules will operate and then revert to normal in the evening. You need to have dinner ready to be heated up. It might be the only thing planned on the day. If it's just for you, you can have a number of dinners-for-one in the freezer, or if you have to cook for others, you could do an all-in-one casserole at the weekend and freeze some for your Day Off.

So, on Whatever You Feel Like Days, go where the feeling takes you. By doing that, you remind yourself that you *do* feel and are not tied to the clock. Obeying your instinct is not always easy; you have to be mindful, and listen to what your body is saying. For example, I have learned that if I start to pace around, I need to get out and walk around somewhere where there are people. Sometimes you feel like having a huge fry-up for breakfast, and sometimes you feel overwhelmingly tired. Just attend to the paramount need...then, when that has been attended to, a new need will emerge. The whole day will seem like an effortless sequence of enjoyable activity.

In retrospect, you could say that you may have done some of the same things if you'd been in planning mode and put them on a list. True, but the elements of surprise and exploration would be missing. Quite an achievement to feel all day as if you were on holiday in your familiar local environment!

We are so used to ignoring how we feel and ploughing on at work, that on a Day Off we must do what our body tells us. This is not a new invention. I remember my mum confessing to me that when she used to have an afternoon to herself when we are all under five and my grandma would take us to the park, she would collapse on a chair and read for the whole time except for the last quarter of an hour when she would rush around doing everything required of her. It was probably the second day of the casserole.

Too Tired

Whatever you Feel Like philosophy can equally apply to a Day Off when you feel really tired. This is a day when you are not ill and off sick but just have no energy and need to recover. You may have taken the day off for this purpose, anticipating you'll be tired, for example after a particularly stressful week at work, staying up all night to watch a baseball tournament on TV, going to an all-night party, or returning from a long-haul flight, or even after a long weekend away.

Alternatively, you may have planned a full Day Off of one kind or another but on the day feel so weak that you can't put any of your activities into action. My daughter recently told me she'd planned a Day Off at the shops and had a really well worked-out list of clothes she needed. After the first hour she was exhausted and just gave up on it; she obviously needed rest not activity. She salvaged the rest of the day by watching videos in bed but did feel a bit sorry for herself by the end of it.

This is a day when you may not even get up. You may have your dressing gown on all day and fetch food from the kitchen when you need it. You do not want to have to talk to anyone nor have any external interference to your thought processes. Maybe you're recovering from some particularly stressful episode at work or unconsciously terrified of something that is about to hit you when you get back. The reason you feel tired doesn't matter; it's good that you've recognised it. On a day like this you are a million miles from the normal things that happen at work. If by mistake you had your work phone switched on and you answered it you'd be horrified. Here's an example of doing what you feel like because you are very tired.

Doing Very Little

"Instinctively you know how energetic you are as the day begins. I woke up on my regular day off feeling like a lump of lead and designated the day as a Tired Day, no questions asked. As I find it quite hard to be lazy, to let myself be tired was a learning experience: I managed to recover without getting too bored and despondent. I had tea and then breakfast in bed, reading a little bit of a magazine. Then in my pyjamas I managed to empty the dishwasher…easy does it! Collecting the mail and a random pile of undealt-with business, I retreated to bed to go through items idly, reading about unwanted offers, looking at my pay-packet and bank-statement. By this time I felt so drowsy, I removed them to the floor and cleared the bed. Too tired to read, I fetched my facial cleansing kit and eye make-up remover and treated myself to a thoroughly relaxed cleanse and tone. I also got up and did a soothing eye-bath and came back to bed. I managed then to look through my notebook, slowly tearing out old lists and putting things in my diary. It was comforting to feel just *slightly* in touch with reality.

Believe it or not it was nearly lunch-time. Still in pyjamas, I went down and put a washing in while heating up some soup and brought lunch up to bed and watched the news on TV. I read my book for ten minutes and fell asleep for half an hour. When I awoke I felt better but not amazing. What easy thing could I do? Wandering downstairs I found some seed packets and managed to read the the instructions and think vaguely about where they could go in the garden. Next I read what to watch on TV that night. It was 3.00pm. I felt I really ought to get up. I put on loose clothes and did some pottering in the kitchen and moved the washing on. As it was a sunny day, I sat outside for a while reading. When my husband came home we had a chat and he offered to cook the dinner which I gladly accepted. While he did this, I tidied downstairs. We ate in front of the TV, then watched one of our recorded films. I went to bed at 10.00pm and awoke next day feeling absolutely fine. Looking back, the Whatever You Feel Like Day had worked perfectly!"

Out of Action

Sometimes you are actually constrained to limited activity by an accident. You cannot rush around and are reduced to doing only what your body can take. Last summer I twisted my foot and used my Day-Off to sit down as it was too painful to walk. Instead of cursing that I had so much to do, I decided to try *enjoy* doing absolutely nothing. The doctor had told me just to put the foot up, put a packet of frozen peas on it and take a pain-killer. Here's my report:

"It was cool inside the house and baking hot outside: 31 degrees. We were having the bathroom re-fitted, so the fitter was in there making a terrible noise all morning. Limping about from time to time to talk to him or get food from the kitchen, I spent the day sitting on the settee reading or watching TV. The afternoon was a special treat when Wimbledon came on, the players thrashing about and the audience squinting, red-faced and sweating in the sun while I sat in the cool with the frozen peas. Basically *nothing happened all day.* I was a bit bored and lonely and annoyed that I would now be limping for some time to come. However, the next morning I felt magnificent and limped into work ready to go. I had given my brain and body a rest at the same time...a rare occurrence."

Your whole life is spent worrying. Sometimes your body commands you to listen and obey. On these occasions, you must not worry about a thing. You need to take it easy or you'll be tired all week.

Lesson Learnt

Everybody will have their own way of "going with the flow".

Chapter 2 - Single-focus Days

The first reason to have a single focus in the day is that you have a task, or an issue which is urgent or serious enough to set aside a whole day for. Because we are on the merry-go-round of work, we brush under the carpet many tasks which, if we tacked them successfully, would transform our lives. A Single-focus Day gives us a huge amount of thinking/action time.

You can focus on issues within a range of seriousness. This Chapter covers days when you rationalise some of your possessions, a day when you look at problems in your life/work routines, and a day when you tackle a more serious life-issue. In all cases you are allowing yourself to *stand back* from your normal life, tackle an aspect of it in detail and take corrective action. A day is just the right length of time for standing back. You give yourself a breathing space. Getting to grips with a troublesome aspect of your life in some depth needs time and concentration. When you feel you have cracked a problem or got somewhere at least with it, you can take some follow-up action during the rest of the day or fit action-times into your diary for the future. The main thing is that you dedicate the day to the problem. The final Single-focus Day in this chapter is one in which you are involved in an absorbing leisure activity.

Systems Day

On a plane, listening to the safety instructions, you hear the cabin-crew member say,
"Always fit your own life-jacket before fixing those of your children."

I wondered about the wisdom of this. Surely children need your help first? Then I realised that, although it seems selfish, if you as the adult responsible for the child make yourself safe first, your mind is then free to focus on making the child safe. I felt this could be a general principle in life: operate your own life as efficiently as you can and you will be in a better position to help others.

Your life runs as smoothly as the systems you have

put in place for it.

Your "systems" are your routine procedures which get you through the week. They have evolved to cope with your timetable and you notice them only when they are not working properly. I'm talking about home and work routines and how the two work together. Here are some examples of systems failure and repair.

Defrost the Crisis

You know how long your journey to work takes and normally leave early enough to beat the traffic. You dread snow and ice and suddenly one morning, without warning, there it is! You are unprepared. The man next door is peacefully running his engine while he sits with the blower on the front window and the radio on. You need a quicker solution but where is the de-icer? And the scraper? You feel panicky as you know you will be late for work. It's a horror and you rage that cars can't manage to defrost quickly by themselves. Instead it's a Neanderthal experience of numb hands, sprays and scrapers, exhaust fumes, frost inside the window, frozen wipers. The whole carry-on adds at least 45 minutes to your journey-time and your morning's energy supply is used up by 8.30am. So, on your Systems Day, take time to write down what you can do about it:

- keep an eye on the weather-forecast
- buy a huge supply of de-icer and a scraper
- get up 30 minutes earlier
- buy a windscreen cover and put on the night before
- have a pair of old gloves and hat at the door

That's it then? Problem solved. That didn't take a whole day. No, these are good suggestions, but now you have to act upon them and the good news is that you have free time now to do this.

You make a note for tonight to check tomorrow's weather. You set your alarm 30 minutes earlier. You phone car-shops in your area to ask if they sell windscreen-covers. You decide it will pay off to go out and buy it later today along with the de-icer and scraper if you can't find last year's. After searching in the house, you find the gloves and hat and put them near the front door ready for tomorrow's frost-battle.

You will still have time left. Just choose from the array of related problems which the sudden drop in temperature usually brings. Can your boots cope with icy pavements? Where are your winter scarves and warm underwear? Do you have enough hot chocolate?

Laptop Drag

You may consider that your work issues are off-limits for a Day Off. Perhaps, but work may still prey upon your mind, so it's probably worth doing some proper thinking about your work-routines rather than hoping they will change all by themselves.

If you can take time out to stand back and reflect, it will be worth it in the end: two hours invested on a Systems Day can change things for you for two years. Personally, I find I can always think things out better when I'm at home.

I knew someone once whose systems were always perfectly worked out. While the rest of us were stumbling across pitfalls, discovering this or that didn't work, he had it all worked out…to his own and not necessarily the company's advantage. "Working smart" is the expression I think. Although I detest this calculating approach and am reluctant to apply it, I sometimes sit down and take a look at a failure or persistent irritation which happens every week and ponder on what could be changed to make things work better. A year ago I was annoyed by having to drag a trolley containing my lap-top and paper files to several different sites in the course of one day. The trolley rumbled noisily on the cobbled streets and I couldn't go shopping after work with it in tow.

After two hours of sitting puzzling about how to change my system I came up with some good ideas:
- possibly re-arrange my timetable to work at only one site per day
- request PCs at all sites where we work
- find out how to get my work emails at home

The outcomes from this Systems Day were spectacular. I started to work at only one site per day, and my request for PCs at all sites was eventually heeded, which benefited everybody. I managed to get my emails at home and the trolley was banished from my life. This was not done by magic however. Again, there was the intermediate step of taking action on every one of the good ideas:

- rearrange timetable, 1 hour

- draft the text of the formal request for PCs to Head of Operations, email and copy to Line Manager and Team Leader, 1 hour

- make appointment with IT assistant to help me access emails at home, 15 minutes

All of this was done in my free time that day. You can see how devoting a Day Off to a work issue now and again pays off in the long-term.

Many employees have been on training courses and learnt business techniques which are transferable to their private lives. The technique used in the example above is "brainstorming". The trainer stands up front with a flip-chart and writes down all the ideas coming from the group. In this way a problem can be explored in depth and suggestions for solutions gathered. You can quite easily do this by yourself with a pencil and A4 pad. It is a way of making conscious what is worrying you and what you can do about it.

No time for Exercise

You can't seem to fit any exercise into your week. You decide that swimming would be good and that the only possible time is Thursday after work. You have put the swimming kit in the boot, but eight weeks have now passed without a visit to the leisure centre. Today you are going to use your Systems Day to brainstorm why. You begin to write down a number of problems:

- feel weak and hungry on the way home so can't face it
- hair always in a mess afterwards
- put off by the thought of struggling in and out of clothes
- swimming costume too old and too tight
- get back late and then have to cook
- sometimes there's a meeting after work

You write down a number of possible solutions as they pop into your head:

- quick snack before the swim or something to munch in the car afterwards
- wash hair properly next morning

- take sports clothes to change into

- buy a new to-die-for swimsuit

- have a ready meal every Thursday

- occasionally miss the swim when there's a meeting

The snack is appealing and you need a new swim-suit for your holiday anyway; you don't mind ready-meals, but the sports clothes, the changing and the hair may be too much after a day's work. Nevertheless, you decide to give it a trial run. You cannot buy the swim-suit until next week but today you can go and buy your snacks and ready-meals. As you drive into town to the supermarket past the leisure centre it occurs to you that you could have a swim on your Day Off. Now there must be a reason you don't. Possibly it could be that you *do* want regular exercise but you *don't* want all your Days Off to be the same. Fair enough. No one can say you haven't persevered with the swimming idea, and Thursdays still may work.

It is very satisfying to use the tail-end of a good Systems Day to put your thinking into action by finding or buying essential equipment to make the new system work. Recently I went out and bought a huge supply of pencils with rubbers on the end because I could never find a rubber. They are now in my desk-drawer and I feel so comforted when I see them.

Lesson Learnt

Writing down hitches in your working and personal routines magically suggests possible solutions.

Let's Face It Day

Face what? Well obviously not a minor thing, like clearing out the garden shed. Facing up to a really knotty problem in your life requires at least a day to make headway. Surely it would take longer than a day if it's really serious? It may take a lot longer, but the Let's Face It Day is the first time you look it in the eye. How long have you been worried about a particular problem and, because of its difficulty, never got round to doing anything about it? Here is your chance. Focussing for a day on a *single issue which is important to you* means clearing everyday activities out of the way and being alone and undisturbed. The issue you may want to tackle could come under the heading of Finances, Relationship, Career, Living Accommodation, Health. Here are a few examples of serious issues and how you can begin to resolve them by taking a day to face up to them. These examples are chosen only to illustrate the techniques you would use to deal with them: you will know what, if any, are *your* serious issues at any time. You will see how the simple act of writing ideas down can help you organise your thoughts and move forward.

Financial Issue

Let's look at the scenario of a working woman in her forties, who is in a bad situation financially. She has been separated from her husband for two years but has not yet filed for divorce. It's not easy to untangle the problems as she nears the precipice of losing the small flat she has recently taken out a mortgage on. She has not made any claim on her share of the family home where her husband is still living. As the relationship is definitely over, she needs make an appointment with a solicitor, file for divorce, and send her husband the letter. She is going round in circles. Various fears are holding her back. She doesn't know where to start.

On her Day Off, having a ready meal in the freezer, she will get herself a coffee, sit down with a pencil and A4 pad and write down:
What am I worried about?
She will put her fears down one by one. At a certain point, she will break off and look determined, as some of her fears suddenly seem smaller than her own long-term insecurity. Lots of things she will now have to do have become as clear as day.

She will need another page to jot some of these down. When she has discovered more actions she needs to take, she then has to think out the order in which to do them and the blocks of time she will have to fit them in. Will it be on another Day-Off quite soon, or can some be done during a weekend or after work? She might even have time to do some of these tasks today, BUT, as the focus of this day is thinking and planning, it may be better to allocate future time slots to some of the actions. Otherwise, she could get bogged down in one problem and lose the longer-term strategy.

I wonder how far she would have got without actually writing things down.

Career Issue

We all jog along in our jobs and hope we can keep ourselves happy but then a Let's Face It point is reached. Just say you have been unhappy at work for some time. Your colleagues have got used to your negative tone and you have been buying smart clothes as a way of cheering yourself up. On your Let's Face It Day you decide to take it on.

You need an A4 pad. Just start writing.

Begin: I am unhappy at work because….

and see what comes out. Like the previous example, you are using a technique normally used in a professional context called *brainstorming.* Its purpose is to produce a field of ideas relevant to a problem and it is used within a group of people. Substitute yourself for the group and off you go! What comes out might be 2 lines or 3 pages. If it's short, it means you are so wound up, you can't open up even to yourself, even now when you have a whole day available. You've written for example:

- I hate that office. It's a horrible place. I want to escape. I hate my work. I don't want to go back ever again but I need the money. I'm trapped.

To open up more, try becoming your own counsellor. Take it bit by bit, asking questions:

- *What do you hate about it?*

- I hate the stupid hot desks, the open plan, the idiotic rules about the kitchen, the endless meetings, the long afternoons, the office manager and her favourites......
Your counsellor stops you…

- *You've only mentioned one person so far....is there nobody you like in the office and can talk to?*

- Oh! Yes. We're all friendly and have been there for quite a while; I can talk to them.

- *So is it your manager who is the real problem? Tell me more about this manager.*

- Right. OK. She seems to have it in for me…..
Aha! Now you've opened up! You can now write pages, asking yourself questions as you go. A trick is

to ask yourself *open questions,* in other words, questions which start with a question word, *who?, what?, why?, how?*, rather than *closed questions, like "Do you ...?* to which the answer can only be "yes" or "no". Open questions help you answer much more in the one go, so you get to the heart of the problem faster. Again this is a technique of questioning used in the counselling and careers-advising professions which is quite easy to use on yourself. For example, you could continue:

- *Why do you think the manager has it in for you?*
- *How do your qualifications compare with the rest of the staff on your level?*
- *What would you feel about being moved up to a higher level?*
- *How would you view a sideways move?*
- *How would you feel about studying further in your spare time?*
- *How could you improve how you feel in your current job?*

This last question is a key one. In times of recession when jobs are scarce, our chances of moving upward are limited. For this scenario we need to be more resourceful in keeping ourselves happy.

At the end of this searching process, you will have a better idea of why you are so unhappy and have resolved on some timed action to improve your situation. If you have time left, the rest of the day is yours to enjoy. You will be having positive and happy thoughts as if a weight has been lifted from your shoulders. And you will have done all this entirely by yourself!

Health Issue

Life seems such a treadmill. Just say that you are in reasonable health but never feel really healthy. You sense that your eating habits are partly the problem and want to do something about it and break the cycle. A Let's Face It Day is perfect for breaking into bad cycles of all kinds. If you take time to think out what is wrong and what steps you will take to correct it, you will feel more in control. You are going to take time to look at your diet, I don't mean that you're necessarily *on* a diet.

You've got the whole day ahead. Where do you

start? To review where you're at, write on your A4 pad,

My Current Eating Habits

and write down a few points about your physical heath related to food at the moment, e.g.

- drinking too much tea and coffee
- feeling hungry at 4.00pm
- eating too much at evening meal
- eating chocolates in the evening
- sleeping badly

Look at these in turn and see if you can root out the cause of this merry-go-round. Why are you hungry at 4.00PM? You do not eat enough at lunch-time as you have had a snack at 10.00AM. Why? Because you don't have breakfast and get hungry mid-morning...

The problems you bring to the surface when you consciously write them all down will magically suggest their own solutions. The brainstorm could be less than an hour out of your day but action-points will have emerged, for example:

- have a light breakfast even if you don't feel hungry
- buy better quality bread for your sandwiches to fill

you up at lunch-time

- brush your teeth in the evening straight after dinner and spend an hour on non-TV activities to stop you snacking: for example, listen to music, read, have a bath, play a computer game

- reduce your caffeine intake by drinking green tea after 4.00pm instead of normal tea/coffee

When you've got your Action List, you could spend another part of your Let's Face It Day researching where to find wholesome bread and maybe buying several loaves to freeze, as well as buying green tea-bags and putting some in your handbag.

Your Own Health Review

Another Let's Face It Day could take us even further with our general health. We could all be healthier. Unfortunately, the advice we get from the media constantly contradicts itself and we may have given up on believing any of it. Lurking at the back of our minds may be the thought than we *do* know best about our bodies since we live in them, and it is within our power to experiment on some aspect of our lifestyle in order to feel better and more energetic. We all have aches and pains but maybe nothing serious enough to go to the doctor about.

You can do your own Health Review. Just start at the top of your body and think your way down. So, hair, head, face, ears, eyes, nose, neck and so on right down to toes and stop and write down any area that has been bothering you. You may be surprised at the number of problems you find. You might have put down *eyes*, and *feet:* your eyes are often dry and itchy and your feet hurt in certain shoes. Take the most serious first. Say it's the feet. Just make a note of what sort of pain it is and when you notice it. How long is it since you went to the podiatrist? Do you even know of one? Again, you will suddenly think of what you need to do about it. So write it down and you may even be able to do it today.

By the end of the day you may have made an appointment with a podiatrist to have your feet checked, taking your shoes with you. About the eye problem, you may have called in at a chemist for advice and bought suitable eye-drops.
Perhaps a single Let's Face It Day will not complete

the Health Check, and you'll use another one soon, but at least you have made a start.

The searchlight of my head-to-feet check once shone on my teeth. Not a pretty sight: when I smiled there was a huge gap bottom left. I made an appointment at the dentist who told me dental implants were the only solution and were extremely expensive. After a few months of dithering, I designated a Let's Face It Day to make a decision one way or the other. On my A4 page, I did a quick *pros and cons* analysis:

For: improved appearance, chewing food better
Against: horror of imagining what the dentist is
doing, pain and discomfort, time off work, cost

That day, I made the decision in principle to have the treatment. To me, the two positive reasons to go ahead seemed to outweigh the four negatives. I felt so wonderful and brave about making the decision that I didn't bother to work out the details of cost, time off work and so on. Eventually, I managed another Let's Face It Day to work out these details and succeeded in setting the whole thing in motion. I now have a lovely smile and enjoy my food more. You often look back and wonder why it took you so long to make a really good decision. It is usually because of the pressures of life and work!

We have looked at examples of relatively serious issues which have been tackled successfully in the time and space afforded by a Let's Face It Day. You can see that really important decisions cannot be made while your mind is trapped by the routine of work. A Let's Face it Day allows you to focus on one issue at a time and resolve it.

I have shown how writing things down is essential to help you think. Problem-solving techniques like brainstorming, open-questioning and pros and cons discussion, normally used only in professional contexts, can be adapted for self-use to sort out your problems. These techniques now fall under the umbrella of Self-Counselling, easily searchable on the internet.

Lesson Learnt

Being honest with yourself about serious problems becomes easier if you write them down.

Clear-out Day

This Single-focus Day is more straightforward,
physically oriented and easier on the brain than the
previous two. The Chapter is divided into two parts,
the first relating to general clearing-out and the
second to dealing with your clothes. Clear-out Days
are the necessary groundwork for Shopping Days.
They are an audit of your possessions which allows
you to see what can be thrown out to make room for
what you need to buy.

General Clearing-out

It is therapeutic to clear things out now and again.
Once you get into clearing-out mode, you can get
carried away, so that's why this day is in the Single-
focus category, but you could equally well clear out
just one cupboard as part of a Patchwork day if you
are very disciplined.

Although *clearing* is different from *cleaning,* the
two naturally go together. I think that the type of

household maintenance which you do at weekends just to keep your living space respectable is truly boring: tidying up, cleaning surfaces, vacuuming. Much more satisfying is the type when you go behind the scenes, get stuck in to very cluttered places and have to clear and clean at the same time. Here are two reports and an example from Clear-out Days.

Chain of Tasks

"The intended clearing areas were my make-up drawer and the items under the bed. These lasted most of the morning, and made me realise that the bedroom was deeply dusty. So in the afternoon I set to, vacuuming properly, cleaning windows and paint-work, dusting, and washing the net-curtains …I also found some kitchen nets to wash. Moving to the kitchen I found a cupboard with food well past its sell-by date, threw most of the contents away, cleaned it and made a list of replacement items to buy. I then found that the dish-rack was gruesomely filthy so put it in the bath to soak. While in the bathroom I noticed that the bath taps were covered in a film of white, so attacked this with lime scale-remover. In the late afternoon I was all cleaned out. I had really got into the mood but had used up every ounce of my energy. I enjoyed the clearing/cleaning, especially moving from room to room in a chain of tasks. One thing does lead to another on a day like this. Of course there was no dinner made and I still had to put the nets back."

What could the end of a Clear-out Day look like? Well, you need to stop before you get too tired. There is always a temptation to do *more* rather than less: resist it. You may then be able to go to the dump or a charity-shop with bags of things you've thrown out, or you could buy something pretty for the area you've cleared, like flowers or some nice soap. Alternatively, you could sit down and don't get up except to put the ready-meal in the microwave.

Sweat the Small Stuff

"I have just cleared out the sideboard drawer. This is the woman's equivalent to a *man-drawer* where you put any object you have not really got a place for over a period of time. You really have to sit down on the floor for this job. If you haven't got a place for these objects they will all have to go back in, won't they?

Birds of the British Isles cards, bronze paper-knife

castors, coasters, curtain-hooks

elastic bands, endless post-its

key-rings, Kings and Queens of England cards

mouth-organ

paper-clips, pencils, pens which don't work,

peppermints

plastic watch from a quality Christmas cracker

and a string mouse which the cat is too old to play

with

(I've just thought...this could be put to music!)

Because there were so many other places for things to go and I kept changing my mind, I began to write post-its for separate piles of things, then finally took them away to their new destinations. The bin should feature strongly as a destination when clearing. A thankless task, except that finding the bird-cards helped me identify the new bird threatening the others in the snowy garden. And the drawer is now emptier and ready to be filled up again."

Face your Past

In many ways, clearing objects is easier than clearing

paper-work. The older you are the more files you will have: insurance, household bills, past jobs, previous hobbies, medical files. Their contents have to be read before you can safely throw anything away. It is much more comforting just to leave them unopened for long periods, BUT the time comes when you need the space they are taking up, or you are looking for particular things and can't find them.

It can be painful too. All those years ago, you kept those training-notes thinking they'd come in useful and now they look really out-dated as times have changed. Sometimes you do come across something interesting which makes you pleased with your previous performance, or reminds you of a pleasant patch in your life.

Again, as you go along, you can use post-its to indicate the destination of separate piles of papers: "keep in file", "throw out", "put in another file". In the interests of staying sane and keeping a balance of active and sitting tasks in a Clear-out Day, I'd say two hours on files is enough. You will be pleased with the space you've saved and may want to treat yourself to some new stylish box-files which look good on open shelving.

Clear-out Days certainly make you feel good *but not until the next day.* On your way out to work you will enjoy the clear space where there was a clutter, or find in the sideboard drawer a pen which works. But be careful about one thing and you will be back to endless drudgery if you forget this: before the Clear-out Day is over, every item must be packed up in a bag with a label...no, you can't just leave piles of objects on the floor for the time being. Do not leave jobs unfinished, for at the end of the working day you will not be in the mood to deal with them.

Clothes Sort-out

Sorting through your clothes requires more time than normal clearing because you have to try things on. A Clothes Sort-out gives you the chance to discover what your immediate needs are. By the end of the Clothes Sort-out Day you will have written a list of important items to buy.

On this day you are going to focus only on your clothes. Do you think that Henry V111 ever had to have to sort out his clothes? No he did not, because he had an army of wardrobe people to do this for him. So for the day, you will function as a clothes-support team for yourself. Like Henry, you need to look your best in a number of contexts and time is required to produce this result.

Unfortunately, you may feel like dashing out to the shops the moment you open the wardrobe door, but a shopping fix is not the answer. Instead, you are going to review what's in your wardrobe to discover important gaps, and garments which are of no use to you.

Triggers for a Clothes Sort-out Day

If you love clothes, you may not need triggers because you sort out your clothes quite frequently and easily. However human nature dictates that we mainly respond to immediate needs and don't look too far ahead at any one time. Generally I am jolted into wardrobe-action by having a special occasion to attend or the season changing but any of the following situations could suggest it's time for a sort-out:

-your drawers are full up yet you only wear a quarter of what's in there

-you are going on holiday

-you have put on weight or lost weight

Suddenly It's Summer

Sometimes summer starts suddenly without warning. One day last year I thought I had no summer work-clothes. I pencilled in next my Day Off to look them out. To inspire me, I bought my favourite glossy magazine ready for the day. Here is how the day went:

"Had I bought summer clothes last year? Where were they now? Under the bed? Yes. I got them out and tried them on. Some were fine. Some had been there for years unworn. Trying them on showed the various reasons why....unflattering, too tight, too young- or old-looking. They had to go. I resolved to buy more in the styles which did suit me. Having done this for work clothes, I fished out my collection of summer leisure clothes. Surprisingly some were still nice but there were no decent shorts nor lightweight trousers and only a few decent tops, so these went on the list. My bikinis made me look dreadful. I bravely resolved to try on a different style on the Clothes Shopping Day.

At lunch-time, I ate a sandwich while reading the fashion sections of the magazine and noted down some shops with possible trousers to look at. I returned to the bedroom which was by now full of heaps of clothes. This is when I did my change-over from winter to summer: I put all the decent winter things in the boxes under the bed and brought out the summer ones to hang in the wardrobe or put in the drawers. Left on the floor was the heap of rejected summer and winter clothes. I had no hesitation in getting rid of them. So, into the black bin-bag they went. I still had time to get them straight off the premises....always a mistake to leave the bag lying about and go back on your decisions! Off to the charity shop they went. A great feeling of relief followed and then I could shop for new things."

Clothes can be rejected for lots of reasons. It

doesn't matter: you don't want them clogging up your storage space. If you take clothes into a charity shop the majority of them can be resold cheaply to others who want them. Some people find it easier to keep than throw away. The argument with clothes used to be that *they may come back into fashion!* Vintage shops now sell all these really old clothes to young people. The useful life of your clothes is extended by giving them away, and if you want vintage you can always buy it. I keep only a very small number of garments from the ancient past. They will never fit me again. I loved them then and love them now, and take them out occasionally to look at.

Keep trying: you're worth it!

Devoting a A Day Off to your wardrobe at any time of the year can save you time and money. If, instead of trying on my summer things first, I'd gone straight out to the shops and bought lots of random summer items, forgetting what I had already under bed, chances are I would have come home with a number of duplicate items. For many women, it's a reflex action: sun comes out, off you go to buy cheap T shirts. Don't buy new T shirts just because you're going on holiday. A friend of mine counted 37 the last time she looked in her drawer.

You could dedicate part of a Clothes Sort-out to going through your underwear, socks, tights and pyjamas and shoes. Are you uncomfortable, too hot, too cold? Changed bra-size? Clear out your drawers, trying on all the while. Footwear is often the most difficult to decide on. Fashions change all the time and shoes and boots need to work well with a number of outfits. How many pairs of sandals are in the storage boxes under the bed? Why were they no good last year? As you go along reviewing your clothes and looking ahead, have a notebook and pencil ready to write down exactly what decisions you've come to about what to buy. At the end of a thoroughly hard-working Clothes Sort-out, you feel you have earned your Clothes Shopping Day. (See Chapter 3).

Lesson Learnt

The day feels therapeutic because it serves both as a prompt to future material needs and a way to retrieve objects and memories from the past.

Get Absorbed Day

So far our Single-focus Days have been very different from our work-routine but scarily and obsessively related to our *maintenance or holding our lives together.* Where does inspiration come in? Can we ever hope to get a break from our normal preoccupations? At the end of a good Day Off we will feel better organised, with our affairs more under control, but will we have been reminded of what *really* matters to us, what we enjoy most about the world we live in?

One day, when I had not had my weekly Day Off for very long, I admitted to myself that so far I had seldom had more than a few moments of feeling inspired. I had lots to do but did not feel like doing it and yet had nothing set up for me to escape into. My mind drifted to something a friend had said the week before about being "completely absorbed". I sat down and wrote out what she'd said.

In a Different World

"I was speaking to Hannah about a Life Drawing

Class she had started going to. She said she couldn't remember when she'd been so utterly absorbed in something. I understood what she meant: while puzzling why the arm was wrong or how to make the foot really stand on the ground, her mind had left its usual circuit and she had been in a different world for three hours. This took her away from work and home issues: it was a true rest for the mind. Physical exercise can also take your mind off your usual worries. Although some people may be able to fit a regular fitness session, sport or yoga class into their working week, not everybody is in a position to to so. I began to think I really needed a way to become absorbed, and envied those who managed to achieve this."

Pondering on my envy, I remembered having the same feeling in relation to a teacher friend of mine. One sunny day on my Day Off I went to have tea with Lesley. It was the Easter holidays and I would have expected her to have had lots of time to chat, but teachers cannot choose their days off, so when their holidays start they go berserk with the rest of their lives. She was too polite to say, but really she was far too busy to sit down and talk. I made my own tea. Her normally tidy kitchen was in a total mess, covered in scraped off paint while she applied paint-stripper to an old table. She was quite happy in the temporary mess and enjoying skills revived from some time in her past. I remember being envious of her and reflecting that I probably had never got stuck in to a practical project like this but would have liked to. It would be so relaxing to get lost in something and stop my brain going round in circles.

You can plod on and get so far from your sources of pleasure that you forget that they exist. So to keep in touch with your capacity for intrinsic enjoyment it's best to programme in times when you will feed it. I'd say that to keep a balance between going overboard with inspiration and never allowing yourself to open the door to it at all, *you need to allocate inspiration-time on every Day Off you take* and this can be anything from ten minutes to the full seven hours.

Habitual Escape

So, can we use a Single Focus Day to be become absorbed? Or is it too short a time? Obviously my friend Lesley had practical skills. Also, being on her own required her to do all the D.I.Y in the house.

I asked another friend who now has a regular Day Off how she spends her time. She said her favourite activity was cooking. She uses the time to cook and freeze dishes ahead for the family, and bakes for a Saturday charity stall. I imagined her warm kitchen smelling of apple tarts, surfaces strewn with ingredients, her face smudged with flour...and again felt wonder and envy.

Personalities differ and there are many sources of absorption. A friend at work makes greeting-cards and now and again will take a day off to prepare a new batch. My sister-in-law knows how to alter clothes and will occasionally devote a day to this. People who have gardens may spend lots of Days Off digging, planting and weeding. My friend with the horses neglects her garden and goes riding. All of these hobbies were established earlier in life and so are now easy to go back to in one's free time. The secret is to have the tools of your trade set up before the Day Off begins. If your hobby or activity is on-going, you will have your equipment ready to hand and can pick up where you left off.

I know of young men who can get absorbed for an entire day on the internet, in computer games or exploring the applications on their smart phone. They will say that it is the accidental discoveries they make that are the fascination and they are transported from the 9-5 into not one, but into many different worlds.

Here's where I admit that throughout my life I had always kept a journal of experiences and thoughts important to me, and gradually realised that the activity which would be sure to inspire and engage me on my Day Off would be writing a book about it!

I've Always Wanted to ...

Many people will have a secret inkling that they'd be good at an activity, e.g. badminton or woodwork, and are just waiting for a time to try it out. Alternatively, they have always put off researching something they really want to know more about. Could a Day Off be a chance to start something new? Because the Day Off is a neutral period of time and your mind can feel free, sometimes you find yourself able to open the door to an absorbing activity.

A friend told me how she had made her plans for a great outdoor day, involving lots of physical activity, and woke up to the rain bucketing down. Looking out of the window, she was not content just to go round and create an indoor list. She heard an inner voice whisper, "Your ancestry, go on, do it. An ideal chance. This is the moment. You have put off for long enough. Go on. Just do it."

On her family tree was a great-grandmother with a non-British surname. She knew roughly when she would have died. She went on to an ancestry site, paid her subscription and, to her amazement found the grandmother in the first five minutes, discovered that she was Turkish and had several brothers and sisters. She looked at the clock. It was still only 9.30AM! Time had actually slowed down. For the rest of the morning she continued researching, and by lunch-time could phone her mum to tell her what she had found out. Was this better than digging the garden or clearing out your drawers? She felt such relief that she'd got started at last..now she's got a project! She'll continue at weekends and on several Days Off. You can see that when circumstances interfere with your plans this often allows you to go off in an a more unusual direction, even lead to a breakthrough of some kind.

New Career Direction?

If you are frustrated at work, you might wonder if you could use a series of Days Off to pioneer a new direction for yourself. During a Let's Face it Day, you could have decided that instead of being a corporate slave you want to develop ideas for a business of your own. Web-site design comes to mind: many designers teach themselves, start designing for friends or small businesses and find that this becomes a career.

However you'd have to plan carefully. Occasional Days Off will not provide enough time to change career and you'd have to down-size from full-time work in order to get the new business established.

But you could begin to brainstorm your new business on a Day Off. Say that you want to research buying hats on the internet because you always dreamt of having a hat shop. You spend part of three Days Off just surfing various hat web-sites. On the fourth occasion you go off to visit a successful vintage clothes shop. The next time, you have other things to do, and the time after that you need to prepare for going on holiday. Will you be able to fit in the continuation of your interest every week? If you feel it's an important departure for you, make sure that you do. Every week you need to touch base with your project or it will gradually fade away into an ex-project and you will be sad to hear yourself talking about it as if it were still going on when in reality you have given it up. To avoid this happening, always record your progress in a journal or scrap-book or computer-file, making notes of what you have learned and what you need to do next. If it turns out to be impossible to pursue your idea at the time, you can return to your file for inspiration in the future and be re-inspired.

I hope you will use Get Absorbed Days to follow your inspiration to the depth that time allows, but don't be annoyed with yourself if you lapse. After all, if you are reasonably well suited to your current job, this is where your income and a decent level of absorption comes from for now, and you can't have everything! Having said that, as we have seen, during Day Off time, you could easily revive a a former interest or stumble across a new project which could be the basis of a new career or something to take up seriously at a later point in life.

Lesson Learnt

Recording your progress with an activity which absorbs you will help you take it up again in the future.

Chapter 3 - Shopping Days

Following on from your Clear-out Day, with its two parts for general and clothes, here are the two parallel types of shopping day you will enjoy as a result of your clearing efforts. Before I became a Day Off expert, assuming that all shopping was the same, I used to shop for clothes and non-clothes on the same day. After a few frustrating and exhausting Shopping Days I concluded that that you must have two types, Clothes and Non-Clothes. This is why I have put them under two different headings. Of course, the general advice in this first section applies to clothes shopping too...because shopping is shopping.

Mixed Shopping Day

This is a Day Off when you are going to buy bigger and more important items than in your weekly food-shop. I am aware that patterns are changing as supermarkets stock larger household items and people shop for *everything* on-line, but most of us still love and need to walk around specialist shops or department stores from time to time. Having a whole day to look around, choose and buy, is a splendid luxury, but this is a purposeful and not a dreamy kind of day. I have had good and bad days in town and I have learnt how to maximize the chances of a good one.

Just because you have allocated a Day Off, it doesn't mean you have to use it all: you could start early and finish at lunch-time or spend the morning planning and resting and head off in the afternoon. Starting early, if you can force yourself, gives a wonderful feeling as you walk freely around empty shops and streets and it is lovely to go home knowing you will have time to recover. Starting late means there are more people around and before you know it, the schools are out and it feels like the end of the day.

Lists and Dead-lines

You will have made a list over several weeks, having had Clear-Out Days in which you discover and make an ongoing list of what you need, for example, new everyday cutlery, a shower curtain, a food-mixer. I use the personal organiser on my 'phone or write my ongoing list in pencil on the front page of a spiral bound notebook and then rub out items when I've bought them, making room for more. It is always good to bring your longer list but also write a short list of just those items you aim to buy on the day. Alongside these, list the shops most likely to have them, and for a further refinement, re-write the list in *shop order* repeating all the items you propose to look at in each store, otherwise, you will succeed in buying one thing, leave the shop, then remember the others!

It is useful to have a deadline. At the start of a day you know how much energy you've got and what it feels like when you overdo it. None of these purchases is a matter of life and death. Just work out an end-time and stick to it. It helps if you have to catch a bus or train and this sets the deadline. Car-parking is expensive. For years I have paid little attention to the tariffs and once spent £12.50! It was my son who made me think of money and time together: he said he had managed to buy eight things in one hour because he wanted to spend only £2.00 in the car-park! A good lesson. I now spend less on parking and shop faster and more efficiently.

Look Good and Be Comfortable

It's amazing how shop assistants are pleasanter to you if you feel you look nice. For shopping, it's important to go out wearing clothes you love. At the same time, shoes and clothes must be comfortable or you can't concentrate. It's better to risk being slightly cold as you speed from shop to shop than sweating your way round or carrying your coat.

Most Difficult First

When you are not sure exactly what type of food-mixer you want and need to look around a bit, there is a case for getting on with it first thing. You may research on-line first to save time, but feel you need to see and handle the goods, and search in more than one shop. So put this at the top of the list. Time and energy are in short supply and if you still haven't decided after an hour, it is time to leave it and get the easier things.

Rest and Eat

You should try to keep to your normal routine even on a shopping day...your body expects it! I started my last shopping day with a a big almond biscuit and cappuccino...something which cost nearly £5.00, but it was 10.30AM and I was hungry. Lunchtime could go to 2.00PM but better stop earlier if that's what you do at work. It can be tempting to gobble your lunch as you can't wait to get to the next shop but it's better to relax a bit and take your time. Sitting down with your healthy sandwich and hot chocolate, you can observe others and their troubles and keep a sense of balance, or you can immerse yourself in reading. Rather than carry a magazine or newspaper around all day, before setting off I cut out an article I haven't had time to read and read it over lunch.

Battle Campaign

If you accept that shopping is hard work and aim to plan your campaign, you should have success and arrive home with all your purchases, time to spare and a sense of achievement. However, beyond being prepared, there is no accounting for success or failure on the day. Sometimes luck is with you, sometimes it isn't. You may go to have a new battery put in your watch and it costs twice as much as you thought, or it may cost roughly what you expect and you are given a voucher for a free coffee while it's being done!

Continuous Improvement

Life is for learning. As well as knowing what's in the shops, every time you shop you will learn something about yourself, your moods, your comfort-zone. I don't think that people who have time to make shopping a way of life are necessarily better shoppers. Those of us for whom time and money are scarce make the best shoppers and are hopefully happier for it.

Lesson Learnt

It's better to treat the day like a military operation than a pleasure-trip.

Clothes Shopping Day

Clothes shopping needs to be done separately because of the level of emotion attached to how we look. In the course of the day, we experience more extreme highs and lows trying on clothes than we do searching for household items. I believe that a different part of the brain is used for clothes buying. You can prove this by trying to look at table lamps after a morning in the fashion shops: you really don't care. And if you try to do it the other way round, leaving the fashion shops until the after the table-lamps, chances are you will be too tired for this super-demanding activity. Once the quest for beautiful clothes starts, it gets hold of you. As workers, we seldom find time to devote a whole day to clothes shopping. It's usually the lunch-hour dash and another day returning things which didn't suit. I'm sure some of us have a stab at it every weekend, sometimes with others.

My view is that a Clothes Shopping Day has to be a no-nonsense day. It is not about browsing nor hanging out with friends; it's serious trying and buying. You do *not* need someone with you. I've seen too many men drooping on the chairs in large fashion outlets. I find it's best to drop him off somewhere. There are even pubs advertising themselves as

Husband Drop-Offs. Many women involve their partners in the decision-making, the men often paying lip-service when really they have no interest whatsoever. So consider going by yourself. How do you measure success on such a day? Everybody does it their own way. I have learnt to focus on what I really need but not be too disappointed when I don't find it. Given how difficult it is to choose clothes which make us look good, I have provided a few examples here of difficulties from my own experience and suggestions of how to do better.

Two Birds with One Stone

In two weeks' time you have a wedding to attend; you've got the outfit but need the accessories. You also have a party this weekend and maybe the wedding shoes can also go with the outfit for the party. You've got your list compiled you've got one day to get as much of it as you can, like a trolley-dash. There are five items: shoes, bag, wrap, earrings, necklace, and you have made a list of probable shops.

You are not wearing the dress but you know what

will look good with it. You start by looking for shoes because they will be the most difficult, noting bags at the same time. Trying on shoes is hard work. Six shops later you really are despairing of finding the perfect shoes : some would cripple you and some are just not wedding-friendly. You feel like one of the ugly sisters. It's at this point also that you become hungry and have sore feet even in your "comfortable shoes". You tell yourself not to despair: you're doing all the right things. It's time to sit down, have a light lunch. Give yourself time to reflect.

After lunch you have one last shop to try for the dream shoes but you have a sinking feeling you won't find them there. This is the worst part of the day. So here comes the compromise. Face up to it and you'll feel better. You've tried on a pair which are not exactly comfortable but might be OK....*provided you have time to wear them in.....* but are maybe not what you'd call *wedding* shoes. Well, too bad! They will just have to do. Who defines what is and isn't a pair of wedding shoes? Your outfit is gorgeous. Who's looking at your feet? Does the style go with the dress?

Yes. And would they also be OK for the party? Yes? Right! Your Fairy Godmother says you should try them again.

Off you go, full of resolve, try again, and decide to buy. That done, a matching bag is available. You're on a roll, and the wrap suddenly appears also. Phew! A sudden exhaustion comes over you from the relief but you have still to get your jewellery. OK, time to get a coffee and rest.

The hit from the coffee goes straight to your decision-making brain. You will go straight to your most likely jewellery-shop and score a direct hit. Success! Things *are* looking up: you see just the perfect necklace and earrings *and they are on sale!* Feeling pleased with yourself, you call it a day. Ignoring the lovely top you glimpse out of the corner of your eye, you arrive at the car park in good spirits and drive home. You've done a brilliant job. Get ready for the usual comments from your partner about all the time and money you've spent. Just laugh it off. In fact you have been economical *and* your success has put you in a good mood, so, brilliant! When you get home, you've still got time to try the accessories with the outfit and model the ensemble for your partner...well, *somebody* has to watch! Was that a good Day Off or what?

I'm afraid you never really know until the next day. During the night you wake up with something on your mind. It's one of the purchases, the key one in fact, the wedding shoes! They are supposed to be comfortable. They *look* comfortable but pinch your big toe in a serious way..in fact you're in pain even now having walked around in them all evening at home. In the morning the truth becomes clear: they will not do. How could you have made such a mistake? Immediately, you know what to do: use your lunch-hour to take them back and find a pair of sparkly sandals instead for the wedding. You may have to take back the other accessories another time and change your plans for the party.

Trying to kill two birds with one stone was a bad mistake. You started out with the aim of buying *one pair of shoes when you really needed two*! To fulfil this aim you ended up with a pair of uncomfortable shoes, no good for either occasion and a bag and wrap of the wrong colour. You thought you were saving time and money. Really, it would have been easier to buy one pair for the wedding and forget the party. Wedding gear is like that...it's hard to wear again except to another wedding. And shopping for *two* pairs of shoes in one day!! It is tempting to try to double up purchases in this way when you are generally pushed for time. I remember wishing I had a Clothes Shopping Day every week. In fact in the early days of having a regular Day Off, I did spend all of them in the shops, making mistakes! One solution to trying to do too much and getting it wrong is possibly just to shop for ONE item and not stop until you find it. Let's see how that goes.

Single Garment Mission

You dive into town. It's a Single Garment Mission. For a long time you've wanted a jacket...lightweight, with texture or pattern, pockets, to be worn outside in summer but inside, for example in a pub. You know just the places to try. Full of hope, you try them one by one. Your heart leaps as you see a window full of jackets..then sinks as you see they have no pockets. This makes you see red. Would a *man* ever have a jacket with no pockets? You know how your mother would respond to that one, and imagine the whole conversation with her:

"No, but *he* doesn't have a hand-bag, dear."

"No, and he doesn't have a handbag because of the extra hassle a handbag is. Men would have invented handbags for themselves if they had been necessary. Men's jackets have *lots of pockets.*"

"You're right. It's not fair, dear, but let's get back to your jacket: a couple of reasonable pockets will do, won't they?"

"Yes, mum."

Gloom has set in, but you carry on looking for the "art-jacket" with pockets. Mmm, you are seeing lots of other delicious garments out of the corner of your eye, but that always happens on a one-garment mission. The last shop is reached. Will you buy ANY jacket now? No, because you have managed without it for so long anyway. The awful truth dawns that there are no suitable jackets in the last shop: the unsuitable ones hang dejected, slighted by your indifference, and it's all over. You go through a short period of mourning, and then your heart lifts as you find a new café where you can sit outside and watch the shoppers on their way back to the station. Now hear this: no fewer than four women of your age, chatting happily to their companions, walk past wearing just the sort of jacket you have been looking for.

"Stop!" you would like to shout. Where did you get that jacket? I didn't see it!"

But then you remember Murphy's Law of the fashion world which says that when you covet something another woman is wearing and ask where she got it she will usually say she's had it a couple of years or she bought it in Germany. So, the jacket was not to be. Not for now anyway. You don't even want to think about it.

This single-garment mission did not work out, for reasons which we could go into: the season, range of stock in the shops, looking for something very particular, or again, like the shoes, possibly trying to force two jackets into one. You just have to feel the defeat sometimes. But, to avoid coming home completely empty-handed, alongside a particular item, *you could have put another couple of things on the list.* These could be accessories, jewellery, or underwear. By closing your eyes to everything but jackets, you disallow the possibility that something else will catch your eye. Clothes buying is not an exact science as you know, and here are some other danger-zones for the unwary shopper.

Falling In Love

Sometimes you see something you are not looking for and don't need. It can happen any time in life, with clothes too, that you just fall in love. If you buy it on impulse without trying it on you will return it and put it down to a false attraction. But if you do try it on and it loves you too, that's hard to resist. Believe it or not, I have some tips for you here.

If it is well above your expected price-range, you'd have to think quickly about the sorts of places you'd wear it. I have a dress which likes me but when I put it on I always feel too dressed up, so it hardly gets out. And is the beautiful garment hanging beside other extremely expensive items meant to co-ordinate with it? You really need to look at these as a whole because this is actually someone's clever mix-and-match wardrobe. Is it yours? Can you afford it? You should consider perhaps one item to team up with it. Once I bought a dress for a party. It had a perfect little jacket on the model, but did I buy it? No, and a year later I found myself buying something similar just to replace the thought of it. Even worse, I bought a beautiful pair of black Italian evening trousers, perfect fit, and decided against the matching fitted sleeveless top in the same material. What a mistake! Every time I put on the trousers, I feel the need for the top, like a lover whom I had let go. All right, if you insist that you must buy the one beloved item, at least force yourself to think what you have at home to wear with it.

Sales Are Dangerous

You need a lot of time and energy for sales. Most of us are not sales-watchers. We just like a bargain, but basically all these clothes on the Reductions rail, if it is a genuine sale, are the ones people did not want. In the past I puzzled over every item and often ended up ended up walking out. There is a reason *not* to buy every garment. I have a really expensive designer dress bought from a sale rail. It is a feather-light summer dress of black muslin which cost me only £35.00. I now realise why no-one bought it: it is black. As we wear dark colours a lot in winter, when the sun eventually does come out, black is probably not what we are looking for. If you can, avoid the sales. It is far better to plan ahead: look early on at what's coming in and be ahead of the game.

Now, you will be fed up with all these tips and annoyed at me for reminding you how tough and time-consuming it can be to find what suits you in your price-range. So it's time to look at the other side of the picture. Is there not an case for *just looking* ? Many of us just look because we love the shops and we love clothes in all their shapes and colours. You need this sometimes.

Just-Looking Mode

I was inspired to consider this contrasting type of activity by my sister-in-law. She said she frees herself from the normal purposeful clothes shopping mentality from time to time and thinks of the day as a free exploration of shops in town...to do whatever she wants. However, she feels she has to start by aiming to buy one easy item which she knows she will get, like tights. She hangs the day on the tights so to speak. Having bought these, she goes wandering off and doesn't know where she will go or what she will do. She feels as light as air as she wafts though coloured scarves, tinkles shiny bangles, breathes in new perfumes, sifts through underwear. She really is just looking. She walks into shops she doesn't usually go into, finds new ones. The shops become a treasure trove. And you don't have to buy anything!

To get into this mode, it is better not to *need* anything urgently. You also have to be in the mood to drift and muse and be relaxed enough not to be aware of time passing. If you get tired, you rest. You will probably end up somewhere you didn't expect and do something you've never done, like having a manicure. Basically, this is a Whatever You Feel Like Day, applied to the fashion shops. The benefits will be general and spiritual, not tied to any other cause. Of course you *may* buy a small thing or make a note of something you'd like to look at again!

Lesson Learnt

If you are clear about what you need you'll minimize disappointment and mistakes but you can never eliminate them completely.

Chapter 4 - Proper Days Out

At last, a proper Day Out! You thought all Days Off were Days Out, didn't you? Well, here we are at last. You are going to go somewhere different for a whole day, far enough to feel it's an adventure but near enough to get there and back comfortably. Why is it so easy to stay in and hard to go out? Admittedly, you only have a single day, and you have so much else to do, but it's worth the trouble to now and again to make the effort. A Day Out, like a holiday, has to be planned ahead or it won't happen. When it's in the diary you can look forward to it.

A Day Out can be spent completely or partly with others, or on your own. So where will you go? Some would love to go to a Steam Museum, others to a Sea Life Centre. Some yearn for the sea at any time of year, others come to life when they get inside an old church or the old part of a town or an art gallery. The sudden hissing of steam, the open mouths of fish, the smell of old plaster or the feel of the cobbles under your feet could all be the trigger to make you wonder, re-engage with part of the living or man-made world. Have you researched which of these attractions are within your travel range in a day? You can make a pilgrimage to any of these places and take the whole day over it.

Day Out With Others

The most relaxing and comfortable Day Out will be with someone you're close to, because you know and understand each other. Very busy people treasure this easy carefree type of day and feel guilty that it cannot be arranged more often. One of my work colleagues has got it all sewn up...she goes out with the same friend once a month to a garden or museum because that's what they like. However, it can be quite difficult to find somebody who will take a Day Off on the same day as you. Your partner's holiday availability may not be as flexible as your own.

Living in the country now, I find towns very attractive for a Day Out. Even if you don't know in detail what you want to do once you're there, make a date with a friend and stick to it and the activities of the day can be negotiated when you meet. If you are both short of time, you can give each other an hour, say, to go off and shop for what you need, then spend the rest of the time together. If your Day out is with someone you don't know so well, I'd suggest a lunch-date first to see how you hit it off, because your Day Off is precious.

Even with friends you know well, a lunch-date is preferable so you can have time to yourself also. Recently I took the train to a town I rarely visit nowadays, to meet two friends who still work there. I set off early in order to do a few things before meeting for lunch. When you're on the train and it takes only 20 minutes you wonder why you don't go more often, or why you don't continue to the even bigger town down the line. It was a changeable May day and I was glad of my warm coat walking from the station into town, but then the sun suddenly came out, tearing a patch of blue sky, and the black glass building opposite suddenly reflected the street, the people, the clouds moving..it was magic. Definitely coffee time. I chose the coffee shop in the book store and read a newspaper in peace. I only needed two things, a birthday card and a handbag. The card was easy but the bag was not: by lunchtime I had scoured the likely shops without success so gave up on it. Searching for the bag was the most dispiriting part of the day. I met my old colleagues and we had a lovely lunch and chat in a place which they knew had just opened.

After this, I went with one of them on a walk, seeing all the building developments since I'd been there and hearing about how my friend's work had changed. Later we found a large pub facing the park and sat outside as the weather had become warm and sunny. Here my friend reflected what a lovely spot this was and wondered why she had not discovered it before.

The main point was that we were both having an experience contrasting with the usual and were refreshed by it. We stayed so late that I missed my train and had to sit on the draughty platform but I didn't care. I felt elated, just enjoying being alive.

Finally on the train home, reflecting on the good parts of the day I suddenly remembered the bad part, the hand-bag search, which had made me tired and depressed.

Drop The Shops

Here's where you learn that the more you shop the less you explore. The purpose of finding the bag interferes with the pure enjoyment of discovery or re-discovery. Confine shopping to Shopping Day and just hang loose on your Day Out. It is strange though, isn't it, that sometimes, in an unfamiliar town, the very thing you've been looking for turns up! You don't want to push your luck by actively looking because as soon as you go into shopping mode the spell is broken.

I made this mistake on another occasion on my Day Off, when I accepted a chance of a Day Out to Cambridge with my husband who had a business meeting. I had two hours on my own. What a fabulous chance to shop! I clutched my shopping-list hoping that new shops would bring success. Set free, I suddenly felt terribly tired. I just could not face battling through crowds of students and tourists searching for what I wanted in unfamiliar shops. Although disappointed at this missed opportunity, I followed my instincts. I felt like sitting down with a coffee and a snack and reading a newspaper. I didn't have to walk far to find this. I gratefully collapsed, and spent a happy half-hour. The luxury of reading a newspaper in a café is one of life's great pleasures. Refreshed but still not in shopping mood, I just wanted to walk and maybe sit down again later. The day was changing from shopping to exploring.

If you don't want shops, you can enjoy walking around finding streets you don't know. I love doing this. When you've walked far enough one way, you go back to base and try another route. Although *not going in* anywhere, like museums or churches, you nevertheless notice where they are located and this will be useful for another visit. You can even write the discoveries in your notebook ready for next time.

   With still half an hour to go, I made it my business to find a place to sit down...which can be hard nowadays and makes our towns and cities exhausting places to be. During the walk I looked up at the decorations on the old buildings instead of into shop-windows and saw lots of interesting stone carvings and crests. I finally found steps down to the river and a peaceful bench to sit on, then made my way back to the car-park to meet my husband. Exploring is more inspiring than shopping can ever be!

Lesson Learnt

Exploring is more fun if it isn't mixed with shopping.

Explore By Yourself Day

Those of you lucky enough to live in or within striking distance of London or any other large city are spoilt for choice when it comes to a Day Out. We are such creatures of habit, though, that I bet you nearly always meet the same friends and go to the same place for lunch. This is fine if the talk is more important than the walk, in other words if you're really there for the companionship and the the place is less important. You see this in films a lot. There is a beautiful scene, autumn in a park with shady trees and rustling leaves, and there go the two characters, heads down, discussing their difficult relationship, completely oblivious to the beauty around them. They scarcely notice where they are.

Once, on my Day Off, I was off to London to meet a friend at our usual restaurant for lunch, and while I was on the train she phoned to say she had a meeting at work and couldn't make it. She was busy until 8.00PM, which was too late for me. I was completely thrown, felt abandoned and a bit worried about having to entertain myself all day. Having thought about it, it occurred to me that I could keep the lunch-date *with myself* and go to the restaurant at the appointed time. I would meet myself there! This gave me an anchor, because I would be able to pass the time until lunch, then emerge at 2.00 with a new plan of campaign for the afternoon. I had a really thrilling day. I took in an exhibition and Westminster Abbey before lunch, and a film afterwards. I wrote my friend a postcard from a cafe before getting on the train home.

OK, I thought, so all you need is a place and time

arranged ahead...you don't need to book it unless it's likely to be busy...a date with yourself, and the rest of the day will fall into place. I learned from this that it's OK to be on your own. I began to think that I could go anywhere I wanted on my Day Off and a new type of Day Off was born: Explore By Yourself Day.

Sometimes the sun comes up on your Day Off and you just want to go somewhere new. There may be no one around to go with. All your friends are at work. So nine times out of ten you will suppress the urge and just go to your usual haunts. I wonder how many of us spend time talking about the places we'd like to go but don't ever go there. Maybe a Day Off is the right occasion. I have a friend at work who has often mused lovingly about a certain beach that she used to go to as a child. It's only an hour away in the car, yet she never goes there. What is she waiting for? Is she afraid of the reality of the beach eclipsing the memory? In life, you have to make sure you do all those things you yearn for.

A relative of mine has stopped working now, but her family have had children and she looks after them and never gets out on her own. I don't think she has ever been anywhere except to the supermarket by herself. It would not occur to her to explore on her own. But, wait a minute, why shouldn't we explore by ourselves? I think as a nation we feel sorry for people out on their own, but we shouldn't! They are the ones who can choose what they will do and not always have to negotiate with others about it. Exploring is better on your own. So if you feel the urge to go off like this, obey your instinct.

Being on your own all day throws up all sorts of challenges, so planning the day ahead is better than just dashing off. Some of us rely on heavily on partners lot for planning our journeys, so this is a chance to strengthen our own tourist muscles. A day off is too short to have it spoilt by discomfort, like trains being cancelled, road-works, noise, being hungry, finding car-parks. So, to enjoy the day, plan ahead, dress comfortably and take your vital equipment.

My Lucky and Unlucky Day

Last summer, I used one of my Days Off to visit a

city I had never been to. I knew there was a large cathedral which is always a magnet for me. It was a bit strange I admit, coming out of the train into a new place. Talented as I am at losing the way, I immediately asked a railway employee if he could direct me to the city centre. He smiled and gestured, "It's just there!". Talking to people is easy in the U.K. They speak English!

Feeling relaxed and ready for adventure, I and turned into the main street and there was the huge cathedral facing me. I always need a coffee at 10.30 but didn't have enough cash, so, seeing a till in a side-street, I waited behind the woman using it. Unfortunately, there was also a pigeon waiting on the parapet above who chose that very moment to drop a big one one my head!! I shrieked and the woman asked if I was OK. I was not, as I had got pigeon-poo in my hair, jacket, bag and wallet, but I lied, saying I was fine, remembering that I had brought travel wipes...pity I had not brought more cash instead! I wiped as best I could, then, still feeling shaken, made for the nearest café and had a wash and brush-up.

Emerging bedraggled at the counter I asked for a cappuccino and a brownie and felt I had to tell the tale to the waiter, who cheered me up by saying that it is a sign of good luck to be thus treated by a bird, especially if it's on your head!

It was definitely time to see the cathedral. I walked all the way round the inside. The exhibition about Henry V111 was interesting but I was totally entranced by the sun projecting the colours of the stained glass on to the flag-stones. I went out, and made my way round the outside, staring up at the huge buttresses, and taking in the old refectory, ending up back at the main door.

Looking for somewhere to have lunch provided a good chance to see what else there was in the city. Strolling up unfamiliar streets is great fun. I felt like a stranger and enjoyed it. I was really hungry but none of the cafés, pubs nor restaurants appealed to me as a place to have lunch by myself. It was lucky that a large department store appeared. I ate lunch happily and, averting my eyes from the enticing colour-coded fashion section, I exited calmly to continue my exploration. In the afternoon, the place was noisy and dusty with road-works because the city-centre was being restored, so I walked back to the cathedral and since there were no seats outside, sat on the grass. It was sunny, and I wrote two postcards. Confident of the lay-out of the place now, I made my way back to the station and got on the right train at the right time. I had lots of time to read and look out of the window. I felt pleased I had made the effort to make this trip and thought it was an excellent way to spend a Day Off.

Being alone had meant I could please myself but also had to *survive* by myself, which increased my confidence. I didn't have anyone to commiserate with when things went wrong but equally I didn't have to attend to someone else all day. If you do feel lonely in the course of the day, you can comfort yourself by planning to take someone with you next time: you'll know your way around.

Although we are not talking about discovering the source of the Nile, exploring by yourself can give you wonderful feelings of conquering the unknown, surmounting fears of coping alone and the sheer joy of discovering the beauty of landscape and townscape. There are pitfalls however. Although there is no real danger walking alone around in busy towns, I think we probably experience subconscious anxiety in unfamiliar places. So, particularly when exploring by yourself, it is useful to be as prepared as you can to avoid any kind of distress from forgetting vital items or carrying around too much. Large cities are full of workers who do the same things every day. They are pulled on invisible strings and bustle quickly around. Just being among them makes your heart beat faster. You need to be well equipped and know where you are going, or the day could be a wearying instead of thrilling experience.

When I go to London, I rehearse in my head beforehand all the stages of the day: the train, the tube or bus, or walking and then decide what I'll need. It's like mini holiday-planning. Here's my Survival Kit:
- small bottle of water
- snack bar
- travel wipes (your hands get filthy after reading a

newspaper)

- mobile

- fold-away bag

- umbrella

- comb, lipstick, perfume sample

- note-book and pen

- articles cut out to read

- sweets for train home

If in the course of the day if I really need something, of course I can buy it, but this takes time out of the day. Better to make a note of it for Next Time. Most of the above have come from my Next Time lists.

This Day Off completes the range of options. We have tried out days doing lots of activities and others focussed on just one, days based locally and days to shop or to go further afield. I hope that you will feel inspired now to choose your type of day carefully, plan it well and make it work for you. I have encouraged you to think of your Day Off as a precious entity, somehow removed from the daily work-routine, a Kingdom in which you are Supreme Ruler, but, as in life in general, things can go wrong.

In the final chapter, we will face up to this fact.

Lesson Learnt

Planning and being well-equipped are essential but be ready for unexpected lows as well as highs.

Chapter 5 - Days Going Wrong

What on earth could make a Day Off go wrong? I'm not referring here to anything seriously bad, just disappointment, the difference between your expectation for the day and the reality. Our plans may not work out for many reasons and even if we have a plan, we can still suffer from a lack of motivation, the inability to get started. Sometimes the problem is external: the plans of others, the weather or seasonal festivals can affect our intentions. Finally, we ignore the Cinderella Factor of a Day Off at our peril. We will look at these, including examples and reports, and see in some cases how we can remedy what's gone wrong but in others just accept, as in life, and learn from the experience.

Motivational Tricks

We all intend to plan ahead but often your Day Off will start without a plan: you will not have decided what day type it is going to be. Alternatively, you *have* decided and even written out some tasks already, but are not convinced by the items on your list or just not in the mood to do them.

Once, I had designated a Let's Face It Day. It was a work issue, serious enough to put some thought into, even on a Day Off, involving changes to our work conditions, but then I realised I had left the key document at work. I felt annoyed and found it really hard to motivate myself to do anything else. I began by treating myself to cups of tea which I neither wanted nor needed and then went on to the biscuits. I had to pull myself together.

I have already suggested how to repair a Shopping Day which goes wrong, by re-programming. A short spell of planning saves hours of feeling bad. Provided you have the time and space to do this, you don't have to grind on miserably. Here are some suggestions to get you out of the chair.

Open Your Diary

Although I said that you need to get away from work physically and mentally on your Day Off, when you feel lost and unmotivated at home, try this. Open your diary and look at one future work entry. This takes you right back into work-mode for a second, enough to remind yourself that you have a paid job *but that just for today you don't have to do anything.* It's great. Keeps you sane.

Tidy Your Immediate Space

This peaceful little act will stop you fretting and may remind you of other intentions.

Be Kind To Yourself

There is a fine line between being really tired and just a bit lethargic. You can test out which is which at any time by starting your list with the words "you could..." This means you don't *have* to do every item on the list. Just put a circle around the ones you feel you are able to do.

Fix An Event

I am amazed by the power of having a fixed event in the day. Magically, during the time leading up to it you are 100% purposeful! I discovered this one weekend by comparing my ticked lists for the Saturday and Sunday. As it happened, I'd had lots of time available on Saturday as we were not going anywhere but my list was full of ridiculous ticks like "Have a cup of tea." On Sunday there was a long list of substantial activities all ticked! The reason was that *I had to be somewhere by 3.00PM* that day. This trick can work even down to minutes. One day my husband phoned. He was already in town and we agreed to meet there in 20 minutes. The drive is ten minutes. This gave me five minutes to make a plan and five minutes to enact it. I actually sat down and wrote a quick list of what I wanted to get done before leaving the house. It is a known element of good planning that actions must be time-bound and these examples really prove it! So, in an amorphous day of blurry boundaries, fix an event and you will start working to fill the time before it. Arrange to go out at 11.00 am and create a simple purpose for the outing. Write your list for the time up until then, and you will have guaranteed success.

The One Hour Plan

Another approach is to make a plan for the first hour only. Just put down ten really easy but boring things to do. For example, tidy kitchen, clear sink, empty dishwasher, look in fridge, take something out of freezer for dinner, decide on vegetables and dessert, peel potatoes, write shopping list, look up TV programmes, put washing in. After this, your mind will be focussed and you will definitely be out of the chair.

Unavoidable Intrusions

The Plans of Others

"Today was meant to be a Patchwork Day with a treat at the end of it: my husband and I had agreed to go for a drink before dinner when he had finished his work...he had a deadline. The thought of the treat made me braver than usual and I had included some real challenges in the patchwork, things I didn't like doing: putting my photos on to the computer, housework, gardening and paper-work. Sometimes the plans of others cut across your best intentions. Here are examples in two reports.

Flapjacks

I always put the hardest first, so launched into the technical chore. I read the camera book, plugged the camera into the computer, but then the camera didn't light up...whatever! I gazed at the computer screen with its nice software hoping for a miracle but none came. Husband not available to help, so had to leave it. First task failed.

Next, the May sun was blazing, beckoning me out into the garden. Although bright, it was cold outside. It had rained the day before and the ground was muddy. Soon a cloud came over and the wind came up, but I was spurred on by seeing my intrepid neighbour out there in her borders. I thought I could prune the overgrown rambler rose-bush. I hung the washing outside as well. When the first big shower came, I had to get the wet gloves off, fetch the clothes basket, run indoors with the clothes, wait until the rain stopped, then, gloves on again, grapple with dripping and prickly rambler rose, only to be stopped in my tracks by my husband wanting a "conversation" first about how we should deal with the rose-bush. I felt annoyed but carried on with the clothes-peg ritual until it became clear that both tasks were destined to fail. I retreated indoors with a heavy basket of soggy clothes, cold, wet and tired. The Day Off was going badly. Not only this, but then came the news that my husband's deadline was not going to be met and he could not go out for a drink after all! I had to re-programme the day. I had been relying on him for company but had been let down. There was no one else available. I had to carry on on my own. The sun had come out again but I was no longer fooled: basically this was a cold, wet May day and the sun kept coming out just to tease us.

For some reason I hate to do paper-work when the sun is shining, so I didn't do it. I decided the housework could wait also, so settled down to read my book. Something in the book made me think of flapjacks. I wondered if I could get away with making some or would they also turn out wrong? I almost never bake these days. Well, they turned out OK! It was soon time to make the dinner but I was too tired to do it: my husband eventually did it and lit a fire. The rest of the day was spent pottering, eating the dinner and watching T.V. in front of the fire. Now, I don't want to go on about what the moral is here because I don't know. I only noticed that when I gave up trying so hard, things started to improve."

The Electrician

"Today, I knew that the day ahead was a Patchwork Day because I hadn't planned anything else. I got going around the house and wrote a plan with a nice balanced sequence of activities. I was aware that an electrician was coming to look at our broken radiator but presumed my patchwork could cope with this.

When he came, we had a pleasant chat and then he installed himself to start work. I began my first job doing some research on the internet, but I could hear his radio and he was singing along with it, so I couldn't concentrate. I felt he was happy at his work and did not want to ask him to turn it off, but began to get irritated and thought of swapping suddenly to a Clothes-Shopping Day, but wasn't in the mood. I knew it would be easier to get up and *do* things rather than try to *think*, so I did all the active things on the list, had lunch and a rest, and in the afternoon went out to the supermarket but also to the café to read my book. It was a varied day and quite enjoyable. I didn't do any of the thinking activities, but I think too much anyway."

The Weather

On a Day Off, you can create your own reality to a certain extent, but we are all subject to the weather. Just imagine a bright but chilly October day. If it were raining heavily, you would feel happier indoors and not yearn to be outside. If it were a warm summer day, you would definitely aim to be outdoors for a large part of it. Feelings of restlessness caused by the weather can affect your Day Off. Here are two of my reports from last winter which highlight the conflict of whether to resist or give in to the weather.

Brave the Elements

"You've seen the beer advert about men in a tent on the south Pole deciding to go out in 40 below zero when really that is madness. I'm writing this on 12th February. It's been overcast and rainy for two weeks. The days are short and the evenings long and dark. In spite of this, some people feel they want to fight it and behave as if it were a beautiful day. On Friday my friend at work had the afternoon off and was about to leave the office. She felt restless and didn't know what to do. She usually rides her horse every spare moment she gets but thought the field might be too muddy. I suggested going to a really nice delicatessen on her way home to buy a couple of tiny treats, but no, she said she'd done the shopping and didn't need anything. Ignoring my protest that it's not about need, she still looked worried and even said she was getting a headache. Good grief, what should she do? It was obvious. Go home and watch the afternoon film, clear out a drawer, or a food cupboard. That's what we're all dreaming of as we sit at our computer-screens peering and frowning and looking at the clock. But no, she'll fight on. I bet she did go and see to her horse. How different we all are!"

Hibernate

"21st January, hailed on the news recently as being the most depressing day of the year. It started raining at 8.00AM and rained all day. I went out just to show the weather that it cannot stop me following my plan. I needed vital supplies….

As I walked to the shop, wincing at the steady drizzle, I passed the lady down the road, peering out from her huge anorak, pile of twigs in hand, smiling and happy, ready to get the garden cleared ready for spring. Brrr! I don't think so. Winter Days Off are for enjoying your indoor surroundings and belongings. What a mistake it was to have braved the outdoors. The only people you see are those grinning with determination and they're bound to say " Dreadful weather, isn't it!" When I got back and warmed myself up, I looked through some of my lovely summer holiday photos and this reminded me of how short the hibernation season is and how it should be cherished. At 12.30 I had a light lunch as I didn't want to fall asleep. It was so dark I turned the lights on. Cold splashing rain lashed against the windows. I put on an extra sweater. No more brisk walks for me! I carried on with this book-writing project for a bit, then found some indoor tasks on a list, which l did. To accompany the recorded programme I wanted to

watch I made a hot chocolate. As I sat wrapped in a
blanket with my hands cupped around the warm mug,
I could sense my work colleagues out there in the
grisly world struggling through the worst day of the
year and imagined them applauding as I found the
perfect solution to it."

The Seasonal Calendar

The weather guides you towards feasible activities
but seasonal events intrude regularly and force you to
do extra things whether you want to or not. Just think
of the number of birthdays you have bought cards and
presents for, parties organised, May Fairs, summer
fêtes, Guy Fawkes nights. It's not that I want to
obliterate the whole seasonal calendar, but you have
to admit that these events syphon off a great deal of
your time which could be better spent. Most women
throw themselves into Christmas but others would
rather throw themselves in the river. The following
report registers my annoyance with the inevitable
burden of Christmas preparations and suggests a way

to defend yourself.

Clear Yourself an Hour

"This is where I am today 17th December. The whole day could quite easily be consumed by household cleaning, logistics, recipe research, food-and present-shopping, finishing off this or that before Christmas when the brain closes down for a week. Instead of that I am holding back and putting some time into the project of writing this book, which should ultimately be of more lasting value. I'm clearing an hour at least, surrounded by old candles, fairy-light boxes, piles of paper-work, cobwebs and doubtful presents. The patchwork is designed for the rest of the day: a nice jumbo sandwich of sweaty physical activities and sitting thinking things out.

I'm temped to give this book project up right now and abandon myself to The Run Up or Count Down to Christmas preparation, as I've done along with nations of women for as long as I can remember, but I'm not going to, because once you stop doing a project which only gets done on ONE DAY per week, the rot sets in and you can wave goodbye to it. So here we go, one hour on the book before the ascent of Mount Christmas."

There is no doubt that to preserve your own intentions and ambitions you will feel better on your Day Off if you are always strict about limiting the amount of seasonal preparation you do and maintaining the personal activities which give you most satisfaction. For example, last year I managed to make 12 Christmas cards. On my Day Off I had to scrape an hour out of the last-minute rush to clear a space for the cards. I had been thinking about them for so long that I knew exactly how I was going to go about it, and they got done! I was so proud of them and sent them to art-loving friends. I kept one and it is still on my shelf. Seeing the card means more to me than the food that was eaten and the presents I got and gave, the details of which are long forgotten. The home-made cards put me in a good mood and helped me feel festive and enjoy my family's company. And the aftermath of Christmas lasts for *weeks*.

New Year Report

"7th January, Catch Up Day. Here I am, suffering

from a terrible cold, having successfully manoeuvred through Xmas without major mishap. I've completely lost the thread of this book. Christmas takes *six weeks* out of your life preparing for and recovering from the Festive Season. It's not just physical recovery in terms of a return to normal eating and sleeping. Are you really going to stop eating the chocolates before the boxes are all finished? And it's washing the bed-linen, posting off items left by guests, struggling back to work in cold weather, trying to recall your key concerns and projects, putting everything away for another year."

Go with the Flow

Rather than continually reacting to inevitable festivals with anger and resentment, it seems better to acknowledge them and go with the flow, as long as you manage to section off time to maintain your own personal sources of satisfaction. Thankfully in the U.K. there are fewer festivals to celebrate than in other European countries where they all but dominate people's lives. It can be quite exciting on holiday in Spain to stumble upon an exotic Easter parade with its larger-than-life effigies of Christ or the Virgin borne through crowed streets. The minor irritation of traffic jams can be suffered for the glory of the pageant, but if you lived there and had to help prepare for this on your Day Off, attend all day and then host a large family gathering, how would that feel in a yearly cycle of frequent similar events? Bank holidays can fall on your Day Off. If so, I'd surrender the day to a special outing if I were you. Find an event however dull rather than get annoyed that *everybody has the Day Off.*

The Cinderella Factor

Cinderella was warned by her fairy godmother, as you know, that when midnight struck she would have to remember to leave the grand ball. She'd be having such a wonderful time she might just think of staying on, but the magic would suddenly change her back into a kitchen-maid.

Days Off can be ruined if the fairy godmother's warning is ignored. Before you start enjoying yourself, think how the end of the day will look. What is your dead-line? Midnight is a bit late!! If you are responsible for the evening meal, do you know what it is going to be? Rather than think of this later, you could look in the fridge, decide on the meal and quickly do any forward preparation, or, even better, plan on having a ready meal. After an energetic Day Off you will not want to start cooking. Having said that, there are those who can cook at any time, tired or not; they just seem naturally adapted. Their Day Off may often include cooking for fun, including the dinner!

De-brief

The sign of a good Day Off is that your head is in a different place. Following a home-based day, you will be firmly in home mode, comfortable and relaxed. The danger is that you wake up the next day still in this mode and have to drag yourself out of the house. The tell-tale signs are that you find yourself in the morning picking up things from the stairs, putting the books in a neat heap. Stop it! You have to get back into work-mode quickly! No more home-mode, that's it. Out you go.

You may have been out for the day and are in holiday mode, far too inspired. You find yourself selecting a really lovely top for work rather than the usual suspects, but then cannot find anything to wear with it. This makes you late. Perhaps you've had such a successful Shopping Day which went on so late that you haven't managed to try on all your purchases, so you think you'll just try on the skirt and jacket and then realise that it's 8.30!

Rocky Return

It's tempting not to give a single thought to your work-schedule for the next day, but this is extremely hazardous as the following example shows. It's almost as if the distance travelled mentally from your normal work-state has to be made up when you go back. Sometimes you can be so carefree as a result of a great Day Off that you forget the basics and have a terrible return. If the logistics of your working life are variable from day to day you're in more danger of a rocky return than if you work in the same place and do more or less the same work every day.

For example, I recently had a very successful Patchwork Day accomplishing lots and winding down for a nice meal and TV in the evening. The only thing I should have added was a quick glance at my diary for the next day. I *did* know I was going on a morning course, but didn't look at the details until my usual leaving-time. A catalogue of disasters ensued. I was late for the course because I had not left enough time for the journey and did not know my way. In my panic I forgot to take my laptop and folder of work for the afternoon, several important hand-bag items: mobile phone, tissues and umbrella....and it poured with rain. So, especially if you are totally happy at the end of the Day Off, look at your diary the night before to jog your memory about work. You should have feelings similar to a Sunday night, even the negative ones. You've enjoyed the Day Off, used it well, and once you get back to work it won't take long to feel like your normal work-self. You'll relish the companionship of others and value being employed.

You may even brave the kitchen and volunteer a report on your brilliant Day Off.

Printed in Great Britain
by Amazon